PILLARS OF COMMAND

The Core Values of Leadership

PATRICK JESTER

MH

MICHTER HOUSE
PUBLISHING

an imprint of
Rope Swing Publishing

ISBN: 978-1-954058-99-6 (paperback)
ISBN: 978-1-954058-98-9 (ebook)

MH

MICHTER HOUSE
PUBLISHING
an imprint of
Rope Swing Publishing

www.ropeswingpublishing.com

For my loving wife, Carol, who always inspires me to excellence. You are the strength to my weakness! All my love, Hummingbird!

PREFACE

"Fortis Fortuna Adiuvat"

When I was a student at Southern University Law Center in Baton Rouge, Louisiana, I had a pivotal realization about leadership. It wasn't prompted by a professor's lecture or anything I read in a law textbook. Observing the global landscape in 2015, I recognized a profound absence of true leadership. Across the world, we witnessed the downfall of politicians, church leaders, and other public figures. Homes were crumbling due to a lack of effective leadership within the family. This realization deeply influenced me, prompting me to seek the counsel of my trusted pastor, Jay Coleman, the Lead Pastor of Journey Church in Central, LA. Our conversation piqued his interest, and after I poured my heart out, he simply smiled and challenged me with the question, "That's great, Patrick! Now, what are you going to do about it?" Initially taken aback, I wasn't sure how to respond. However, I soon understood that it was a call to action. Accepting the challenge, I committed myself to becoming a dedicated student of leadership. For me to make a real impact, I needed to become well-versed in the principles of leadership. I immersed myself in study, devouring every resource I could find on the subject.

In writing this treatise, my goal was not to compile an exhaustive list of leadership core values. Instead, I have focused on those values that resonate most with me and that I believe lie at the heart of every true leader.

INTRODUCTION

Every person holds values at their core; they are intrinsic to being human and having a soul. These core values are deeply ingrained, requiring no external validation, and are immutable aspects of our identity. They define who we truly are. In leadership, core values are equally crucial, resonating with leaders across all religions, demographics, cultures, industries, and professions. While each core value can stand independently, they are interconnected and complement one another harmoniously.

In the Sermon on the Mount, Jesus emphasized the importance of values, clearly articulating his core values for his disciples. He underscored the leader's responsibility to define core values for those they guide. As someone trained in law, I firmly believe that words carry significant meaning and consequences. Understanding the meaning of a word is essential for grasping its usage in any language. Words have the power to attribute qualities and provide context in dialogue. For this reason, I am inclined to refer to various lexicons, including legal references and modern English usage dictionaries, to gain a deeper understanding of their nuances.

To understand the meaning of Core Values, the root of this term must first be defined:

Val·ue

Pronunciation: /'valyoo/

Plural Noun: values

1. the regard that something is held to deserve; the importance, worth, or usefulness of something.

2. a person's principles or standards of behavior; one's judgment of what is important in life. *(Oxford Languages)*

Core Values are traits or qualities that are not just worthwhile, they represent the deeply held beliefs and core fundamental driving forces of an individual or an organization.

The underlying question of Core Values is, what do I stand for?

INTEGRITY

The Cornerstone of Effective Leadership

In today's rapidly changing world, the concept of leadership integrity has become more crucial than ever. Leaders across various sectors—business, politics, education, and more—are consistently under scrutiny for their actions, intentions, and decisions. Leadership integrity is not just about maintaining ethical standards; it embodies the principles of honesty, accountability, and transparency that define a leader's character and build trust within their teams.

Integrity Defined:

in·teg·ri·ty

Pronunciation: /inˈtegrədē/

Noun

The quality of being **honest** and having strong **moral** principles; **moral** uprightness. *(Oxford Languages)* [2]

You may find it interesting that the only legal authority I have found containing a reference to the word, Integrity says, "See **honesty**." The good news is that in *Garner's Dictionary of Legal Usage*, Third Edition, under honesty, the proper legal usage of integrity is defined as follows:

"Integrity denotes incorruptible **morality** and insistence on meeting not only one's commitments but also one's personal standards of conduct."

Understanding Leadership Integrity

Leadership integrity refers to the adherence to moral and ethical principles by leaders. It encompasses being honest in communication, fair in decision-making, and consistent in behavior. Leaders with integrity act in ways that align with their values, and they hold themselves accountable for their actions. This integrity fosters an environment where team members feel valued and motivated to contribute their best work.

While integrity might seem like a straightforward concept to some, its manifestation in leadership can be complex. It involves not only the personal attributes of the leader leader, but also the organizational culture they cultivate. Leaders must navigate a landscape filled with challenges, pressures, and temptations, all while staying true to their values. The ability to maintain integrity in the face of adversity is what sets exemplary leaders apart.

The Importance of Leadership Integrity

1. *Building Trust:* Trust is the foundation of effective leadership.

When leaders consistently demonstrate integrity, they build strong relationships with their team members, stakeholders, and clients. Most employees are more likely to support leaders who they believe are honest and fair. This trust leads to overall increased collaboration, communication, and ultimately, better organizational performance.

2. *Enhancing Organizational Culture*: A leader's integrity significantly impacts the overall culture of an organization. When leaders prioritize ethical behavior and transparency, it encourages a similar ethos among employees. A culture rooted in integrity fosters open communication, innovation, and accountability, all of which are vital for organizational success.

3. *Attracting and Retaining Talent*: Today, employees are not just looking for competitive salaries; they also seek organizations whose leaders exemplify integrity. Companies led by individuals who prioritize ethical behavior are more likely to attract top

talent. These organizations foster an environment where employees feel safe and respected, making them more likely to stay committed in the long term.

4. *Navigating Challenges*: In times of crisis or challenge, leaders are tested. Integrity becomes especially vital when making difficult decisions that may not please everyone. Leaders who value integrity can navigate these challenges with respect and fairness, earning the confidence of their stakeholders.

5. *Long-term Success*: Organizations led by individuals with integrity tend to achieve sustainable success. While unethical practices may yield short-term gains, they can lead to irreparable damage to reputation and trust in the long run. Integrity-driven leadership focuses on long-term objectives, emphasizing ethical growth over immediate profits.

Cultivating Leadership Integrity

1. *Self-Awareness*: Leaders must engage in self-reflection and understand their values, principles, and biases.

Self-awareness allows leaders to act consistently and transparently, creating a foundation for integrity in their leadership approach.

2. *Lead by Example*: Actions speak louder than words. Leaders who demonstrate integrity in their decision-making and interactions set a clear example for their teams. They must hold themselves accountable in both successes and failures, reinforcing their commitment to ethical leadership.

3. *Create Open Communication*: Encouraging open dialogue fosters a culture of transparency. Leaders should create an environment where team members feel comfortable expressing concerns or providing feedback about ethical dilemmas or decisions.

4. *Ethical Training and Resources*: Providing training on ethics and integrity can help leaders and teams navigate complex situations. Organizations should equip leaders with the tools they need to make ethical decisions and deal with potential conflicts of interest.

5. *Encourage Accountability*: Leaders should encourage accountability at all levels of the organization. This can be achieved by establishing clear expectations, regularly gauging performance, and recognizing behaviors that align with integrity.

Real-World Examples of Leadership Integrity

To better understand what leadership integrity means and looks like, it is important to examine examples from the real-world and from various sectors and industries.

Integrity according to the Boy Scouts of America

Throughout my life, I've had many friends who have been part of the Boy Scouts of America (BSA). While I never had the chance to participate in scouting myself, I hold tremendous respect for the organization's mission. The BSA exemplifies an organization built on the principle of developing leaders who, in turn, cultivate new leaders, perpetuating a cycle of leadership.

One of my friends, Cory Peters, with whom I served on the Board of Directors for the National Conference of Standards Laboratories, International (NCSLI), is a Scoutmaster in the Boy Scouts of America. In 2023, Cory attended a session where I delivered a talk on "The Core Values of Leadership." After my presentation, Cory shared the Boy Scout Oath, demonstrating the alignment of scouting principles with core leadership values.

"On my honor I will do my best to do my duty to God and my country and obey the Scout Law; to help other people at all times; to keep myself physically strong, mentally awake, and morally straight."

Inspired by Cory's sharing, I decided to take a closer look at the values upheld by the Boy Scouts of America. Upon doing so, I discovered that integrity stands as the foremost value emphasized by the BSA.

"As Scouts we are guided by these

values:

Integrity: We act with integrity; we are honest, trustworthy and loyal.

Respect: We have self-respect and respect for others.

Care: We support others and take care of the world in which we live."

Integrity according to the United States Military

I come from a family with a distinguished military heritage. Both of my grandfathers served in the United States Army, as did their siblings, including several of their sisters. My stepfather, Lester Arnold, also served in the Army. Following in their footsteps, my brother Larry and I both joined the United States Army, where our journey in leadership truly began.

Every branch of the United States Military has a deeply rooted set of core values.

According to the *United States Army Field Manual FM 22-100*: The U.S. Army Leadership Field Manual says that leaders who demonstrate integrity: do what is right legally and morally; possess high personal moral standards; are honest in word and deed; show consistently good moral judgment and behavior; and, put being right ahead of being popular.

General Dwight D. Eisenhower said, "The supreme quality for leadership is unquestionably integrity. Without it, no real success is possible, no matter whether it is on a section gang, a football field, in an army, or in an office."

The United States Marine Corps believe that, "...the quality that guides Marines to exemplify the ultimate in ethical and moral behavior; never to lie, cheat, or steal; to abide by an uncompromising code of integrity; to respect human dignity; to have respect and concern for each other."

The United States Air Force says, "Integrity First, Service Before Self, and Excellence In All We Do. These are the Air Force Core Values. Study them...understand them...follow them...

encompass them…and encourage others to do the same."

The United States Navy says in Our Core Attributes that Integrity means our behaviors as individuals and as an organization align with our values as a profession. We actively strengthen each other's resolve to act consistently with our values. As individuals, as teams, and as a Navy, our conduct must always be upright and honorable , both in public and when nobody's looking. (*U.S. Navy – Our Core Attributes* 08 Apr 2020)

During my time in the United States Army, I had the privilege of being led by many remarkable men and women of integrity. Among these leaders, many rose to become senior officers and noncommissioned officers, demonstrating that integrity was their strongest attribute. One exemplary leader who stands out is Jesse W. Martin, First Sergeant, United States Army, Retired. When I was a young Private First Class, Sergeant Martin was my squad leader, and he took me under his wing. As a hardworking Blackhawk Helicopter mechanic, I was passionate about my role, but I struggled to maintain the fitness standards required by the Army, drawing the attention of our company commander.

Sergeant Martin made it his mission to help me meet the Army Physical Fitness standards. He reminded me daily of the commitment I had made to the Army and the importance of honoring it. His dedication to my development was rooted in doing what was right, even in instances where it might have been easier to do otherwise. Jesse Martin is a leader I deeply respect because he consistently prioritized integrity over convenience, always putting his soldiers first. Thanks to his guidance and support, I was promoted to the rank of E-4/Specialist and served an additional four years, eventually becoming a Blackhawk Helicopter Crew Chief. His commitment to integrity profoundly influenced my career and personal growth.

Integrity Exemplified in Christianity

In the Book of Matthew, chapter 6, Jesus instructs us to be cautious about practicing righteousness in front of others merely to gain their admiration. He warns, "If you do, you will have no reward from your Father in Heaven." (Matthew 6:1) Here, Jesus encourages doing what is right for the right reasons, reminding us that while it is natural to appreciate recognition for our good deeds, our actions should not be driven by self-righteous motives, or by a desire for applause.

A poignant example of integrity is found in the story of Philemon in the Bible. To provide some background, during biblical times, slavery was a common practice. Philemon was a slave owner whose bondservant, Onesimus, had fled and subsequently encountered Paul, who was imprisoned for preaching the Gospel of Christ. During his time with Paul, Onesimus converted to Christianity and became a beloved brother in faith. Paul then encouraged

Onesimus to return to Philemon—not only to fulfill his obligation as a bondservant, but because it was the right thing to do.

Choosing integrity, Onesimus heeded Paul's advice, returning to Philemon. What Onesimus did not know was that Paul had written a letter to Philemon, explaining Onesimus's conversion and urging Philemon to forgive him and welcome him back not as a servant but as a brother in Christ. Although Paul could have demanded this out of authority, he made a heartfelt request. Despite having every societal justification to refuse, history tells us that Philemon chose to embrace Onesimus as a brother in Christ.

Philemon exemplifies integrity—doing what is right even when someone has wronged you, especially when societal norms would absolve you if you acted differently. His actions illuminate the profound strength it takes to extend grace and forgiveness, displaying true integrity in challenging circumstances.

Integrity Exemplified in Hindu

In 2023, I had the privilege of speaking at a conference in Tucson, AZ, where I gave a presentation on the Core Values of Leadership. I was deeply moved by the positive response from the attendees, who resonated with the examples I shared on how these core values manifest in various faiths. Many individuals from diverse religious backgrounds approached me to discuss how each core value is reflected in their own beliefs and traditions. One particularly memorable interaction was with my esteemed friend, Dilip Shah, who encouraged me to explore the concept of integrity within the Hindu faith. As with all of Dilip's suggestions, this research proved enlightening.

In Hinduism, integrity is understood as adhering to one's moral and spiritual values, even when faced with pressure to compromise or stray from them. A powerful example of this principle is embodied by Lal Bahadur Shastri, the Prime Minister of India from 1964 to 1966, and a disciple of Mahatma Gandhi. Although Shastri was a Hindu, he upheld the secular ethos of keeping religion and politics separate. His life and legacy are a testament to the core value of integrity.

During his time in prison, Shastri's daughter fell gravely ill. He was granted parole to be with her, but sadly, she passed away shortly after his arrival. Despite having several days remaining on his parole, Shastri chose to return to prison immediately after performing his daughter's last rites. When questioned about this decision, he simply stated that it was the right thing to do. His actions exemplify the profound commitment to integrity—choosing to uphold one's ethical convictions even in the face of personal loss and societal expectations.

A Life Built on Integrity

How does integrity apply to modern American society? Some might think that in today's fast-paced world, the value of integrity has diminished and is often considered outdated. However, that's far from true.

A compelling example of integrity in contemporary American society is the life of John Glenn, a United States Senator from Ohio. Before his tenure in the Senate, he served as a United States Marine Corps pilot and became a celebrated NASA Mercury and Space Shuttle astronaut. Throughout his illustrious career, John Glenn was known for his unwavering integrity. In his personal life, he was a devoted husband to his wife, Annie Castor, for 73 years until his passing in 2016. While this personal example speaks volumes, Glenn's integrity shone brightly even in the challenging arenas of public service.

A poignant story shared by one of Senator Glenn's assistants highlights his commitment to integrity. On one occasion, an elderly senator, seemingly experiencing cognitive decline, criticized Senator Glenn on the Senate floor over a legislative position related to the Armed Services Committee. Despite the public reprimand, Senator Glenn maintained his composure. Later, when that same senator requested a favor, Glenn graciously accommodated him. When his assistant expressed surprise at Glenn's willingness to assist someone who had just criticized him, Glenn reportedly remarked that the senator "no longer remembered the chewing out, and it did no harm to help him on the matter at hand." (*Remembering John Glenn*, lawmaker 2019)

This story underscores how integrity—acting with kindness and understanding, irrespective of past grievances—remains a powerful and relevant virtue in modern American society. It shows that integrity is not just about adhering to one's principles but also about extending grace and support to others, even when it's challenging.

In the movie, *The Right Stuff Ladd/* WB. (1983), John Glenn is depicted as a man of unwavering virtue, prioritizing his integrity above all else. Although it may be apocryphal, there is a memorable scene where Glenn reprimands his fellow astronauts for their extramarital affairs, arguing that such behavior tarnishes the reputation of the space program. This scene resonates deeply with me, as it embodies the high standards of integrity and respect for marriage that I strive to uphold in my own life.

The Integrity of a Business Icon

Recognized globally by its iconic trademarked logo, General Electric (GE) is one of the world's most esteemed and recognizable brands. For many years, GE was led by Jack Welch, a legendary figure in business leadership. Renowned as a management guru, Welch authored several influential books on leadership and management, which continue to be widely referenced even after his passing in March 2020. Among the many qualities that Welch is admired for, his integrity stands out prominently.

In his memoir, *"Jack: Straight from the Gut"* (Welch & Byrne, 2014), Welch underscores the paramount importance of integrity at GE. He writes, "We never had a corporate meeting where I didn't emphasize integrity in my closing remarks." This commitment to integrity as a core value exemplifies how Welch's leadership principles were rooted in ethical conduct, setting the tone for GE's corporate culture. His unwavering focus on integrity not only defined his tenure at GE but also left a lasting legacy in the business world.

Cautionary Tales of Failure to Lead with Integrity

Learning from the mistakes and failures of others is an invaluable way for leaders to grow and develop. A notorious example of failure in leadership integrity is the Watergate scandal involving a United States President.

In June 1972, a group of burglars was apprehended while breaking into the Democratic National Committee (DNC) headquarters at the Watergate complex in Washington, D.C. These individuals were found to be operatives acting on behalf of then-President Richard Milhous Nixon's re-election campaign. President Nixon's objective was to wiretap the phones and offices of the DNC to gather intelligence on the Democratic Party. The situation worsened when he became personally involved in the attempt to cover up the conspiracy.

The ensuing scandal, which shook the nation, ultimately led President Nixon to resign from office to avoid impeachment, conviction, and removal. The Watergate Scandal remains a cautionary tale, highlighting how greed and a desperate pursuit of power led to corruption and a profound failure to uphold integrity. This event serves as a stark reminder for today's leaders of the critical importance of adhering to ethical principles and the core value of integrity.

Insights on Integrity

In my exploration of integrity as a foundational core value, I frequently encountered the widely recognized definition: "Doing what is right when no one is watching." This phrase is attributed to the esteemed British literary figure and lay theologian, C.S. Lewis. While this captures the essence of integrity, I believe it encompasses even more. To me, integrity means doing what is right even when it is difficult, especially when society might condone doing otherwise.

At the age of fifteen, I embarked on my first job at a commercial laundry plant in Scotia, CA. Bertain's Laundry and Dry Cleaning was perhaps the prime employer for teenagers in our town, and on the morning of my first workday, my father imparted a pivotal lesson in integrity. He advised, "Son, do not do your best because your best may not be good enough. Do it the best it can be done!" His words impressed upon me the importance of doing things the right way, setting the expectation for my actions. This principle of striving for the best possible outcome has become my lifelong guiding creed.

Leadership integrity is crucial for effective leadership and organizational success. In a world where trust is often precarious, leaders who prioritize ethical behavior and transparency can develop resilient teams and organizations. By embodying integrity, leaders not only bolster their own reputation but also inspire others to uphold these ideals, fostering a culture of excellence built on trust and respect. In doing so, they lay the groundwork for sustainable success that benefits everyone involved.

CHARACTER

The Core Value that Speaks the Loudest

Character Defined:

char·ac·ter

Pronunciation: /ker(ə)ktər/

Noun

The mental and moral qualities distinctive to an individual. *(Oxford Languages)*

The Character of a Leader: Building Foundations for Effective Leadership

Leadership is often defined by position, authority, and responsibility; however, it is the character of a leader that truly distinguishes great leaders from the rest. Character encompasses a leader's ethical values, integrity, behavior, and how they relate to others. It is the inner qualities that shine through in their actions and decisions. In a world that constantly changes and presents new challenges, the character of a leader is more critical than ever.

The Importance of Character in Leadership

1. *Trust and Credibility*: Trust is a fundamental component of effective leadership. A leader's character is integral to building trust within a team or organization. When leaders demonstrate honesty, transparency, and consistency in their actions, they foster a sense of credibility. Team members are more likely to follow and respect leaders who they believe share their values and

uphold ethical standards. Trust leads to stronger collaboration, improved morale, and enhanced performance.

2. *Influence on Organizational Culture*: Leaders set the tone for the organizational culture. A leader with a strong character encourages a culture rooted in integrity, respect, and teamwork. They model the behavior they wish to see in others, creating an environment where employees feel safe to express their ideas, take risks, and innovate. When leadership character is prioritized, it cultivates a positive workplace culture, where values align with behaviors and organizational goals.

3. *Navigating Challenges*: Leaders face numerous challenges and difficult decisions throughout their careers. Character provides the moral compass leaders rely on during these times. A strong character helps leaders remain resilient and make ethical decisions even when faced with pressure or adversity. This integrity not only ensures the leader's actions align with their values,

but also inspires confidence and respect from their teams.

4. *Vision and Sustainability*: Great leaders are not only concerned with short-term gains; they focus on the long-term sustainability of their organizations. This vision requires a character that prioritizes ethical decision-making and social responsibility. Leaders who consider the broader impact of their decisions on employees, communities, and the environment are more likely to build lasting success. They understand that character-driven decisions can lead to better outcomes for all stakeholders.

5. *Mentorship and Development*: Leaders with strong character often take on the role of mentors. They nurture the growth and development of others, providing guidance and support to help individuals realize their potential. By being role models, character-driven leaders inspire the next generation of leaders to also prioritize ethics, responsibility, and inclusivity.

Core Traits Reflecting Leadership Character

1. *Integrity*:

Integrity is the bedrock of character. A leader who demonstrates integrity acts consistently, adheres to their values, and takes responsibility for their decisions and actions. They do what is right, even when it is difficult or unpopular.

2. *Empathy*:

An effective leader understands and shares the feelings of others. Empathy allows leaders to build strong relationships, foster teamwork, and create an inclusive workplace where everyone feels valued.

3. *Resilience*:

Leadership can often be challenging. A resilient leader remains steadfast in the face of difficulties, adapting to changes and recovering from setbacks. This resilience inspires others to approach challenges with a positive mindset.

4. *Vision*:

Great leaders possess the ability to look beyond immediate tasks and foresee the bigger picture. They communicate a clear vision that motivates and aligns their teams toward shared goals.

5. *Humility*:

Many humble leaders value the contributions of others and are open to feedback. They do not let their position cloud their perspective and are willing to admit mistakes and learn from them, fostering a collaborative environment.

Ways to Develop Leadership Character

1. *Self-Reflection*:

Regularly reflecting on one's values, actions, and decisions helps leaders align their behavior with their character. This introspection promotes self-awareness and encourages personal growth.

2. *Seek Feedback*:

Embracing constructive feedback from peers, subordinates, and mentors allows leaders to understand how their actions are perceived and identify areas for growth.

3. *Commit to Lifelong Learning*:

Character development is an ongoing journey. Leaders should

commit to continuous learning through professional development, attending workshops, and engaging in leadership training.

4. *Model Desired Behaviors*:

Leaders can actively demonstrate the character traits they wish to instill in their teams. Leading by example can inspire others to adopt similar behaviors and values.

5. *Surround themselves with a Supportive Network*:

Engaging with other character-driven individuals cultivates an environment of support and accountability, reinforcing leadership values.

Character According to the United States Military

Regardless of the branch, the United States Military places a high priority on character, viewing it as a fundamental expectation. This strong commitment to character is exemplified by the words of former United States Army General and Chief of Staff, George C. Marshall.

"When you are commanding, leading [soldiers] under conditions where physical exhaustion and privations must be ignored, where the lives of [soldiers] may be sacrificed, then, the efficiency of your leadership will depend only to a minor degree on your tactical ability. It will primarily be determined by your character, your reputation, not much for courage—which will be accepted as a matter of course—but by the previous reputation you have established for fairness, for that high-minded patriotic purpose, that quality of unswerving determination to carry through any military task assigned to you." – General George C. Marshall, Speaking to officer candidates in September 1941

During my time in the United States Army, one of the most impactful leaders I served with offered me this memorable advice: "Have character, Specialist Jester, don't be a character!" –Warner J. Brandenburg, SFC, US Army. He was a true man of character who, although tried hard to hide it, truly cared for those he led. His wisdom has stuck with me as I've grown as a leader, and I strive to impart it to those I mentor. Over the years, many leaders I've engaged with have consistently emphasized that strong moral character is among the most valued traits in individuals, and I wholeheartedly agree.

The United States Army underscores the importance of leadership character, a focus that is thoroughly woven into the fabric of *The U.S. Army Leadership Field Manual*, FM 22-100. The manual provides a comprehensive definition of character, demonstrating the Army's commitment to this fundamental quality.

"Character describes a person's inner strength, the BE of BE, KNOW, DO. Your character helps you know what is right; more than that, it links the knowledge to action. Character gives you the courage to do what is right regardless of the circumstances or the consequences." (*Army Field Manual FM 22-100*, 2007)

The U.S. Marine Corps Marines

take the character of all Marines very seriously! They say that Marines are a "special breed." This reputation was gained and is maintained by a set of enduring core values. These values form the cornerstone, the bedrock, and the heart of our character. They are the guiding beliefs and principles that give us strength, influence our attitudes, and regulate our behavior. (*FMFM 1-0 Marine Corps Manual*)

As professionals, we are defined by our strength of character, respect for others, and a lifelong commitment to Core Values. We all have a responsibility not to engage in—nor tolerate—behaviors that harm members of our formation. (*A Profession of Arms: Our Core Values –* U.S. Air Force 16 May 2022)

When I inquired about the United States Navy's perspective on character, several retired and former Navy personnel emphasized that courage embodies the very essence of the United States Navy's character. This is reflected in the Navy's Core Attributes, which state:, "Courage is the value that gives me the moral and mental strength to do what is right, with confidence and resolution, even in the face of temptation or adversity. I will: Have the courage to meet the demands of my profession, make decisions and act in the best interest of the Department of the Navy and the nation, without regard to personal consequences, overcome all challenges while adhering to the highest standards of personal conduct and decency, be loyal to my nation by ensuring the resources entrusted to me are used in an honest, careful and efficient way." (*U.S. Navy – Our Core Attributes* 08 Apr 2020)

Character Exemplified in Christianity

If character is a true reflection of inner strength, then the prophet Daniel epitomized it in every facet of his life. He demonstrated unwavering integrity by refusing to compromise his values, choosing a diet of vegetables rather than defiling himself with unclean foods. Faced with the daunting task of interpreting King Nebuchadnezzar's dream—a challenge that stumped all Babylonian wise men—Daniel humbly attributed his insight to divine revelation, giving glory and honor to God. Fierce in his commitment to truth, he spoke it boldly to those in power, undeterred by the popularity of his message or the risks involved. Even when praying put his life in jeopardy, Daniel remained devout, steadfast in his faith. Despite rising in favor with the king, his loyalty to his friends and his beliefs never wavered. His life, as detailed in Daniel 2:1-48, is a testament to true courage and fidelity.

A Cautionary Tale of Bad Leadership Character

"What you are stands over you the while, and thunders so that I cannot hear what you say to the contrary" – Ralph Waldo Emerson

Have you ever encountered a leader with poor character? If so, you may have noticed that such individuals tend to be surrounded by others of similarly flawed character. In his influential book, *"The 21 Irrefutable Laws of Leadership,"* John C. Maxwell highlights this phenomenon with Law #9, The Law of Magnetism, which states, "Who you are is who you attract." Leaders with questionable character inevitably attract others who share their undesirable traits.

The Bible offers valuable lessons on this topic, with figures like King Herod Agrippa I serving as cautionary examples of leadership marred by poor character. Herod's reign was marked by egotism and cruelty; he imprisoned Jews to torment them and executed James, who had committed no crime. His penchant for wearing opulent clothing to earn admiration starkly contrasted with his oppressive treatment of the very people he sought to impress. Tragically, Herod's leadership suffered greatly due to his unchecked ego and arrogance.

Character is the cornerstone of effective leadership. Leaders with strong moral character possess that indefinable quality that enables them to succeed. Conversely, those with weak or nonexistent character struggle to inspire others and achieve lasting success. Following a leader of poor character is challenging because it undermines trust and respect.

To avoid the pitfalls of leaders like Herod, one must embrace humility and openness to growth. Acknowledging and confronting personal weaknesses with sincerity is crucial. Surround yourself with individuals of strong moral character, particularly those whose strengths complement your own. Having role models and mentors as accountability partners is invaluable— they have the courage to offer honest feedback where others might not.

According to the Law of Magnetism, leaders with good character naturally attract others who share their moral integrity. Consider John Harris, a servant leader in our Central, LA church. Although not an actor or a famed athlete, John's charisma and integrity are undeniable. Greeting everyone at the front door each Sunday, he stands as a beacon of righteousness and holiness. Those who come to know him are drawn to his high moral standards and either rise to meet them or drift away.

Ultimately, a leader's character is pivotal in shaping their effectiveness and the success of their organization. Character-driven leadership promotes trust, inspires loyalty, and nurtures an ethical culture. As the dynamics of leadership evolve, the intrinsic value of character remains steadfast. Leaders must commit to developing their character, for it is through this inner strength that they will lead with impact, inspire those around them, and forge a lasting legacy.

DUTY

Obligation of Leadership

Duty Defined:

du·ty

Pronunciation: /dōodē/

Noun

1. a moral or legal obligation; a responsibility.

2. a task or action that someone is required to perform. (*Oxford Languages*)

The Duty of a Leader: Guiding with Purpose and Responsibility

In any organization, whether a business, non-profit, or community group, the role of a leader is pivotal. Leadership encompasses various responsibilities and challenges, and the duty of a leader extends far beyond simply directing others. It involves guiding, inspiring, and supporting individuals and teams toward a common goal. Understanding the multifaceted duties of a leader is essential for anyone aspiring to or currently holding a leadership position.

1. *Setting a Vision and Direction:*

One of the primary duties of a leader is to define and communicate a clear vision for the organization. This involves understanding the broader goals and objectives, aligning them with the values of the team, and articulating them in a way that resonates with everyone involved. A compelling vision serves as a roadmap, guiding the team's efforts and providing a sense of purpose.

Leaders should regularly revisit and refine this vision, adapting it to changes in the environment, industry trends, or organizational needs. By doing so, they can ensure that the team remains focused and motivated, fostering a culture of adaptability and long-term thinking.

2. *Empowering and Supporting Others*:

A leader's duty is not only to direct, but also to empower those around them. This means providing team members with the resources, training, and support they need to succeed in their roles. Effective leaders recognize the strengths and weaknesses of their team members and work to develop their skills, encouraging continuous learning and professional growth.

Empowerment involves trust, and leaders must demonstrate confidence in their team's abilities. Allowing individuals to take ownership of their tasks fosters a sense of responsibility and motivation. Also, supporting and mentoring team members creates a positive culture where collaboration and innovation can thrive.

3. *Making Informed Decisions*:

Decision-making is an inherent duty of a leader, and it often comes under significant scrutiny. Leaders must be able to analyze complex situations, consider multiple perspectives, and make informed decisions that align with the organization's values and objectives. This requires a combination of insight, critical thinking, and sometimes, intuition.

In addition to making decisions, leaders have the responsibility to communicate the rationale behind their choices. Transparency in decision-making fosters trust and helps team members understand the "why" behind actions, even when they do not agree with them.

4. *Leading by Example*:

Leaders are expected to model the behavior they wish to see in their teams. Leading by example is a powerful trait that reinforces accountability and moral standards within the organization. When leaders demonstrate integrity, professionalism, and a strong work ethic, they set the tone for the entire team.

Consistency in behavior and values also builds credibility. Employees are more likely to follow a leader they respect and trust, and seeing their leader uphold the same standards creates a culture of mutual respect and accountability.

5. *Fostering a Positive Environment*:

Creating a positive and inclusive work environment is another critical responsibility of a leader. This involves nurturing a culture that values diversity, encourages open communication, and recognizes individual contributions. Leaders should actively seek feedback, listen to their team members, and address any barriers to collaboration.

A healthy work environment not only enhances employee satisfaction but also boosts productivity. When team members feel valued and heard, they are more likely to engage and contribute their best efforts. Additionally, leaders should prioritize the well-being of their team, promoting a work-life balance and a supportive atmosphere.

6. *Navigating Change and Challenges*:

In today's fast-paced world, change is inevitable. Leaders have the duty to guide their teams through transitions while minimizing disruption. This requires effective change management strategies, clear communication, and a supportive approach.

During these challenging times, leaders should provide stability and reassurance. Their ability to remain composed and positive can inspire confidence in their team, helping them to navigate uncertainty with resilience. Encouraging ongoing adaptability and continuous improvement also empowers teams to embrace change rather than resist it.

7. *Accountability and Responsibility*:

Finally, an effective leader must hold themselves accountable for their actions and decisions. Taking ownership of successes and failures sets a powerful example for the entire team. Leaders should also establish mechanisms for accountability within their teams, ensuring that everyone feels responsible for their contributions.

A good leader's duty extends to recognizing the impact of their choices on others. Ethical leadership involves consideration of the consequences of decisions and striving to make choices that benefit both the organization and the individuals within it.

Duty according to the United States Military

"The essence of duty is acting in the absence of orders or directions from others, based on an inner sense of what is morally and professionally right..."

– Gen. John A. Wickham, Jr. - Former Army Chief of Staff

One of the first lessons a United States Service Member learns is that duty and commitment are far more than mere words—they are moral imperatives.

While both concepts involve adhering to a standard, they differ in origin and scope. This distinction is evident in the way branches like the United States Marine Corps and the United States Navy incorporate commitment, rather than duty, into their core values.

During my service in the United States Army, it was ingrained in me that true leadership involves taking initiative. A leader anticipates what needs to be accomplished rather than waiting for instructions. This proactive approach underscores the essence of both duty and commitment, driving effective leadership and fostering a culture of responsibility. What's more, they take full responsibility for their actions and those of their subordinates. Army leaders never shade the truth to make the unit look good—or even to make their subordinates feel good. Instead, they follow their higher duty to the Army and the nation. (*Army Field Manual FM 22-100*: The U.S. Army Leadership Field Manual)

According to the Marine Corps, commitment is the spirit of determination, and dedication found in Marines. It leads to the highest order of discipline for individuals and units. It is the ingredient that enables constant dedication to Corps and country. It inspires the unrelenting determination to achieve victory in every endeavor. (Core Values of the United States Marine Corps)

The Air Force teaches that duty is the obligation to perform what is required for the mission. While our responsibilities are determined by the law,...Air Force instructions, directives, and guidance, our sense of duty is a personal one and bound by the oath of service we take as individuals. Duty sometimes calls for sacrifice in ways no other profession has or will have. Airmen who truly embody service before self consistently choose to make necessary sacrifices to accomplish the mission, and in doing so, we honor those who made such sacrifices before us. (*A Profession of Arms: Our Core*

Values – U.S. Air Force 16 May 2022)

The U.S. Navy emphasizes that the daily responsibility of every individual in the Department of the Navy is to unite as a team to enhance the quality of our work, our people, and ourselves. I will: …Foster respect up and down the chain of command, care for the personal and spiritual well-being of my people, show respect toward all people without regard to race, religion or gender, always strive for positive change and personal improvement, and exhibit the highest degree of moral character, professional excellence, quality, and competence in all that I do. (Department of the Navy Core Values Charter: Commitment)

Duty of leaders in the Bible

The Bible offers several insights into the qualities and duties of a leader, emphasizing principles such as service, integrity, humility, and accountability. Some key biblical perspectives on leadership are:

Servant Leadership

1. Jesus teaches that true leadership is about serving others, stating, "whoever wants to become great among you must be your servant." (Mark 10:42-45)

2. Jesus exemplifies servant leadership by washing the disciples' feet, demonstrating that leaders should humbly serve those they lead. (John 13:13-17)

Humble Leadership

Leaders are urged to do nothing out of selfish ambition or vain conceit, but in humility consider others better than themselves. (Philippians 2:3-4)

Leaders are called to be examples to their flock, avoiding a domineering approach. (1 Peter 5:3)

The duty of a leader is to be like a shepherd. The word communicates love, nurturing, intimacy, and care. (Psalm 23:1-6)

A shepherd's life is spent leading sheep. Sheep are by nature inclined to follow a leader or shepherd. A sheep knows the voice of its shepherd and trusts the shepherd to care for and protect it. In the Christian Church, pastors are shepherds and their congregation are the flock.

Encouragement and Empowerment

Paul encourages leaders to build up those they lead, fostering an environment of mutual support and encouragement. (1 Thessalonians 5:11)

These biblical principles provide a framework for leadership that places great emphasis on service, and focus on the well-being of those we lead, and are aligned with the Bible's teachings on love and justice.

The First Duty of a Leader according to Star Trek: The Next Generation

I must admit, I am an enthusiastic fan of Star Trek: The Next Generation My collection boasts every novel, the full numbered book series, and the complete television series. One of my favorite episodes is "Thine Own Self" from season seven. (*Star Trek: The Next Generation*, 1994, "Thine Own Self") In this episode, Counselor Deanna Troi returns to the ship from her Starfleet Academy class reunion, to find Dr. Beverly Crusher commanding the night shift on the bridge. Deanna questions Beverly on why she chose to become a full commander when her role as Chief Medical Officer didn't necessitate the rank. Beverly explained that she eventually felt the need to challenge herself, admitting that she relished the experience of being in command. Inspired by this, Deanna approaches the First Officer of the Starship Enterprise, Will Riker, expressing her desire to take the Bridge Officer's Test.

After completing most of the test requirements, Deanna finds herself stuck on the engineering portion, which she has failed three times. Following her third attempt, Will visits her in her quarters to inform her that he's halting the test, believing she hasn't made progress toward passing.

Frustrated, Deanna questions whether the test is purely about character or a no-win scenario. Will confirms there is a solution, but insists he can't offer further assistance, emphasizing, "As First Officer, my first duty is to the ship! I cannot allow anyone who is not qualified to be in command of the ship!"

Reflecting on Will's words, Deanna finally grasps the essence of what he meant. She returns to the holographic test scenario for another attempt. In this simulation, the only way to save the ship from impending destruction is to order a fellow shipmate to their death. In that crucial moment, Deanna realizes that leadership often requires making the hardest decisions.

Duty stands as a foundational core value of leadership, embodying the essence of responsibility, commitment, and service. It demands that leaders prioritize the well-being and success of their teams and organizations above personal interests, fostering an environment of trust and mutual respect. By embracing duty, leaders not only fulfill their roles with integrity, but also inspire those around them to act with purpose and dedication. This unwavering commitment to duty ensures that leaders can navigate challenges with resilience and guide their organizations towards sustainable success. As such, duty is not just a value, but a crucial pillar that upholds the very structure of effective and ethical leadership.

CANDOR

The Hard Truth of Leadership

Candor Defined:

can·dor

Pronunciation: /'kander/

Noun

The quality of being open and honest in expression; frankness

The Candor of a Leader: The Power of Honesty in Leadership

In an era where transparency and

trust are paramount, the concept of candor has emerged as a critical attribute for effective leadership. Candor refers to the quality of being open, honest, and straightforward in communication. It encompasses not only the ability to share information transparently but also the willingness to engage in honest conversations—especially when challenges arise. Leaders who practice candor foster an environment of trust, collaboration, and accountability, which can ultimately drive organizational success.

The Importance of Candor in Leadership

1. *Building Trust and Credibility*: Candor is essential in establishing trust between leaders and their teams. When leaders communicate openly and honestly about their thoughts, decisions, and the direction of the organization, team members feel respected and valued. This trust lays the groundwork for strong relationships, enabling more effective teamwork and collaboration.

2. *Encouraging Communication*: A leader who practices candor encourages team members to express their opinions, share ideas, and voice concerns. This open line of communication promotes a culture where everyone feels comfortable contributing, which can lead to greater innovation and problem-solving. In contrast, environments lacking candor often breed uncertainty, speculation, and disengagement.

3. *Enhancing Individual Decision-Making*: Candor allows for thorough discussions regarding opportunities and challenges facing an organization. When leaders are honest about the potential risks and rewards of decisions, they enable their teams to evaluate situations critically and holistically. This collective input often leads to better-informed decisions that take diverse perspectives into account.

4. *Fostering Accountability*: Leaders who practice candor hold themselves and others accountable for their actions and outcomes. This transparency not only

builds confidence in leadership, but also empowers employees to take ownership of their responsibilities. When employees know they and their leaders are openly discussing both successes and failures, it enhances their commitment to the organization's overall mission.

5. *Navigating Change Effectively*: Change is an inevitable aspect of organizational life. Leaders who consistently communicate candidly during transitions can help ease uncertainty and resistance. Honest discussions about the reasons behind change, the impact on employees, and the expected outcomes can promote buy-in and facilitate smoother transitions.

Practicing Candor as a Leader

1. *Be as Transparent as Possible*: Honest communication starts with transparency. Leaders should share relevant information with their teams, including challenges, organizational changes, and goals. While not every detail may be appropriate to share, providing

a clear context fosters an environment where team members understand the organization's direction and their roles in achieving it.

2. *Encourage Feedback*: Promoting a culture of candor involves welcoming feedback from team members. Leaders should actively solicit opinions and perspectives, especially on decisions that affect their teams. This approach signals that the leaders value input and fosters a sense of shared ownership among team members.

3. *Practice Active Listening*: Candor is a two-way street—leaders must not only communicate openly but also listen with the intent to understand. Encouraging team members to share their thoughts, concerns, and ideas creates a reciprocal relationship that reinforces trust and communication.

4. *Address Issues Promptly*: When challenges arise, leaders must handle them with candor. This includes addressing difficult situations directly rather than avoiding them or sugarcoating

the truth. Honest conversations about hurdles faced by the team can lead to collaborative solutions while also demonstrating to employees that their concerns are taken seriously.

5. *Model the Behavior*: Leaders must lead by example when it comes to candor. Sharing personal experiences, including lessons learned from failures, creates an atmosphere where vulnerability is acceptable. This authenticity encourages team members to adopt similar behaviors, thereby reinforcing a culture of openness across the organization.

6. *Create Safe Spaces for Dialogue*: Leaders should cultivate an environment where employees feel safe to express themselves without fear of retribution. This might involve instituting regular check-ins, open-door policies, or feedback forums where team members can speak candidly about their experiences and perceptions.

The Benefits of Candor in Leadership

Organizations led by candid leaders experience numerous advantages, including:

- *Higher Engagement*:

Team members who feel valued and heard are more engaged and motivated to contribute.

- *Greater Innovation*:

Open communication fosters a culture of creativity, where diverse ideas lead to innovative solutions.

- *Improved Morale*:

A transparent environment enhances job satisfaction and morale, reducing turnover rates.

Candor according to the Great Military Leaders

"The day soldiers stop bringing you their problems is the day you have stopped leading them. They have either lost confidence that you can help them or concluded that you do not care. Either case is a failure of leadership." – General Colin Powell

Powell emphasizes the importance of open and honest communication between leaders and their subordinates. Candor is critical for maintaining trust and effective leadership.

Admiral Hyman G. Rickover said, "The truth will set you free, but first it will make you miserable." Rickover's quote underscores the challenging nature of candor, suggesting that, while honesty may initially be difficult, it ultimately leads to better outcomes and freedom.

General James Mattis, known for his forthrightness and leadership style, has often emphasized the importance of candor in military leadership. While there isn't a specific well-known quote of his solely focused on the word "candor," his views can be distilled from various statements and writings. One of his notable insights is:

"I don't lose any sleep at night over the potential for failure. I cannot even spell the word. It's possible to lose tactically and do everything right, provided you don't lie to yourself, and you don't let anyone else around you lie about what's happening."

General Mattis's quote underscores the importance he places on honesty and forthrightness, which are integral to the concept of candor. By advocating for speaking hard truth and awareness of reality, he highlights how crucial it is for leaders to foster an environment where accuracy of information and candid dialogue are prioritized, enabling effective decision-making and strategic clarity.

When doing my research for this book, I sat with my brother, Larry, who is a retired United States Army Master Sergeant, asking what he believes are leadership core values. His number one was Candor. When he said that, I was caught off guard as I did not have that on my list. Larry said that candor is about speaking hard truth to those you lead. More than anything, it is about subordinates being able to speak hard truths to their leaders without fear of reprisal. It took me several months for this to become a reality. Once I grasped the concept of candor, it changed my perspective.

In 2022, I was invited to speak in a panel discussion at the Fluke Corporation's Leadership Conference in Belvedere, Washington. Fluke is one of the foremost leaders in the precision electronic measurement instrument manufacturing world. During the panel discussion, I was asked about my experience as a Fluke customer and my response was candid, to say the least! I told all the people in the room that their service delivery was failing to meet company founder, John Fluke's policy, that "the customer has the right to expect more than they paid for!" At the end of the discussion, I was approached by Fluke President, Jason Waxman, who shook my hand and thanked me for my candor. I was honored to spend a couple of hours with Jason later that evening, where we dove deeper into the issues. It was then that I got what candor really means. Being honest enough to share hard truths with kindness, and constructive criticism, is being candid. Contrast that with sharing hard truths with cruelty, and destructive criticism is being brutal.

Have you ever encountered someone who prided themselves on being brutally honest, yet seemed incapable of offering positive feedback to those they were supposed to lead? I vividly remember one such individual from my career who seemed to relish delivering harsh criticisms. At the time, I had just been promoted to E-4 Specialist in the United States Army and was stationed in Germany, working as a Tactical Transport Helicopter Repairer on a maintenance team. A newly promoted E-5 Sergeant was tasked with leading our team through a periodic phase inspection, essentially a partial rebuild of a UH-60 Blackhawk helicopter. When our platoon sergeant suggested that I join the team, the inexperienced team leader, ignorant of aircraft maintenance and my abilities, declared, "I don't want

Jester on my team! I don't think he has the skill to do a good job!" What this sergeant didn't know was that both my section sergeant, the newly promoted E-6 Staff Sergeant Jesse W. Martin, and our platoon sergeant had worked with me for years and were well aware of my competence. Together, they ensured that the cruelty of an incompetent leader would not prevail, making it clear that his dismissive attitude was unacceptable.

The Bible on Candor

"Candor" signified whiteness or brightness originally. Its etymology traces back to the Latin word "candidus," meaning "white" or "a man dressed in white," which also gives us the word "candidate." In ancient Rome, political aspirants wore white togas to symbolize their intentions. Today, "candor" refers to openness and sincerity—a virtue that is rare yet highly appealing. (*Jefferson, The Candor of Christ*, 2018)

"Let no corrupting talk come out of

your mouths, but only such as is good for building up, as fits the occasion, that it may give grace to those who hear." (Ephesians 4:29 *ESV)*

"Nobody cares how much you know, until they know how much you care." - Theodore Roosevelt

President Theodore Roosevelt's quote emphasizes the realization that the candor of a leader is a powerful attribute that significantly impacts organizational culture and performance. By practicing honesty and openness in communication, leaders build trust, improve decision-making, and foster a culture of accountability. In an age where employees seek authenticity and transparency, the ability to communicate candidly is paramount for leaders who aspire drive their teams toward shared success. Ultimately, leadership candor is not just about sharing information; it is about creating an atmosphere of trust and respect that empowers individuals and drives organizations forward.

ACCOUNTABILITY

The Price of Leadership

Accountability Defined:
ac·count·abil·i·ty
Pronunciation: ə-koun-(t)ə-'bi-lə-tē
Noun
the quality or state of being accountable
especially: an obligation or willingness to accept
responsibility or to account for one's actions

Leadership Accountability: The Pillar of Effective Leadership

In today's complex and ever-evolving world, accountability has emerged as a cornerstone of effective leadership. Leadership accountability extends beyond merely accepting responsibility for one's actions; it involves fostering a culture of ownership, transparency, and trust within an organization. This approach empowers teams, enhances the work environment, and leads to superior organizational outcomes. This article delves into the significance of leadership accountability, its impact on organizations, and strategies for leaders to nurture accountability within their teams.

Understanding Accountability

Leadership accountability involves a leader's commitment to act in harmony with the organization's values, goals, and ethical standards. It includes taking responsibility for decisions, outcomes, and team performance.

When leaders exemplify accountability, they cultivate an environment where team members clearly understand their roles, expectations, and the repercussions of their actions. This encourages individuals to take initiative, make informed decisions, and actively contribute to the organization's success.

The Importance of Accountability

1. *Build Trust and Credibility*: When leaders hold themselves accountable, they foster an atmosphere of trust. Team members are more likely to believe in a leader who takes responsibility for their actions, acknowledges mistakes, and learns from them. This credibility enhances a leader's influence and strengthens relationships within the team, creating a more engaged and motivated workforce.

2. *Enhancing Team Performance*: Accountability has a direct impact on team productivity and performance. When leaders set clear expectations and hold team members accountable

for their responsibilities, it establishes a culture of excellence. Employees understand that their contributions are valued and recognized, encouraging them to perform at their best.

3. *Encourage Transparency*: Leaders who embody accountability foster open lines of communication. When team members feel safe to express concerns, share ideas, and provide feedback, it leads to more collaborative and innovative environments. Transparency in communication not only strengthens teamwork but also ensures that potential issues are addressed proactively.

4. *Drive Continuous Improvement*: Accountability is integral to a culture of continuous improvement. When leaders and team members acknowledge their mistakes and learn from them, they create opportunities for growth. This iterative process encourages innovation and helps the organization adapt to changes while enhancing performance and efficiency.

5. *Promote Ethically Sound Behavior*:

Leadership accountability reinforces ethical behavior within an organization. When leaders model accountability by adhering to ethical standards and holding themselves responsible for their actions, it sets a precedent for others to follow. A culture of accountability discourages unethical behavior and promotes integrity throughout the organization.

Cultivating Accountability as a Leader

1. *Set Clear Expectations*: Effective leaders begin by establishing clear expectations for themselves and their teams. By defining roles, responsibilities, and performance indicators, leaders provide a roadmap for success. Clarity reduces confusion and empowers team members to take ownership of their tasks.

2. *Lead by Example*: Leaders must embody accountability through their actions. By owning their decisions, admitting mistakes, and demonstrating a willingness to learn, leaders inspire

their teams to do the same. Leading by example creates a strong culture of accountability where team members feel empowered to take responsibility for their contributions.

3. *Encourage Open, Honest Dialogue*: Fostering an environment where open communication is encouraged is essential. Leaders should invite feedback, actively listen to their teams, and create safe spaces for discussions about challenges and successes. This transparency helps build trust and encourages individuals to take ownership of their work.

4. *Recognize and Reward Individual Accountability*: Acknowledging and rewarding behaviors that reflect accountability reinforces its importance. Leaders should celebrate team members who take responsibility for their roles and contribute positively to the organization. Recognition motivates others to follow suit and reinforces a culture of accountability.

5. *Implement Individual Consequence*

Management: Holding team members accountable involves addressing performance issues consistently and fairly. Leaders must follow through on commitments and ensure that consequences for actions, both positive and negative, are implemented. This consistency demonstrates that accountability is taken seriously and is a shared value within the organization.

6. *Provide Support for Development*: Leaders should recognize that accountability also involves nurturing growth and development. By offering resources for skill enhancement and personal development, leaders empower their teams to take ownership of their careers and improve their performance. Supporting individuals in their growth increases their commitment to accountability.

Military Leaders on Accountability

In his book, "Extreme Ownership", Jocko Willink says, "Leaders must own everything in their world. There is no one else to blame." Willink, a former Navy SEAL officer, emphasizes the concept of accountability, or Extreme Ownership, stating that true leaders take full responsibility for their actions and the outcomes on their watch.

"Do everything you ask of those you command." – General George S. Patton

General Patton's words reflect the idea that a leader should be accountable for their actions and hold themselves to the same standards they set for others. The concept of do as I say, not as I do, no longer holds. Subordinates will not follow when the leader is not accountable to them in return.

The Bible on Accountability

The Bible addresses the concept of accountability in several passages of the New Testament, placing particular emphasis on personal responsibility and the consequences of our actions. A few of the key scriptures that address accountability are:

1. "So then, each of us will give an

account of ourselves to God." (Romans 14:12)

This verse highlights the understanding that everyone is personally accountable for their actions and decisions before God.

2. "Do not be deceived: God cannot be mocked. A man reaps what he sows. Whoever sows to please their flesh, from the flesh will reap destruction; whoever sows to please the Spirit, from the Spirit will reap eternal life." (Galatians 6:7-8)

In his letter to the Galatians, Paul is speaking to the idea of consequences and accountability, cautioning us that we will be held responsible for our actions

3. "Not many of you should become teachers, my fellow believers, because you know that we who teach will be judged more strictly." James 3:1

In this passage, James emphasized the strict liability that leaders are held to. Greater scrutiny will be placed on leaders and people of influence.

Accountability of Management

Peter Drucker, a respected management consultant and author, held accountability as a fundamental aspect of effective management and leadership. While Drucker provided numerous insights related to accountability, two of the key ideas he championed are:

1. *Personal Responsibility*: Drucker believed that effective leaders must take responsibility for their actions and decisions. He advised leaders to focus on results and to understand that they are accountable for the outcomes of their work.

2. *Delegation and Empowerment*: Drucker was a proponent for delegation of authority and responsibility. His belief that empowering team members to take ownership of the tasks was grounded in the idea of fostering a culture of accountability. People are more likely to commit to goals they help set.

Drucker may not have specific quotes on solely on accountability, but these themes can be found throughout his body of work. This underscores the importance of accountability in achieving organizational excellence and personal effectiveness.

Leadership accountability is a vital component of effective leadership that fosters trust, enhances performance, and promotes ethical behavior within organizations. By cultivating a culture of accountability, leaders not only model responsible behavior but also empower their teams to excel. In an environment where accountability is embraced, organizations can adapt, innovate, and thrive in the face of challenges. Leaders who prioritize accountability create lasting legacies, inspiring their teams to achieve greatness and contribute positively to the success of the organization. In essence, leadership accountability is not just a trait; it is an enduring commitment to responsibility, transparency, and excellence.

CONCLUSION

The Core Values of Leadership serve as the foundation for effective and transformative guidance, establishing principles that inspire trust, foster collaboration, and drive progress. Integrity, Character, Duty, Candor, and Accountability stand out as pivotal values that not only shape a leader's ethos, but also influence the culture and success of the entire organization. By embodying integrity, leaders create environments of trust and transparency. Character enables leaders to connect with their teams on a human level, cultivating a supportive and inclusive atmosphere. Adherence to duty enables the leader to make the tough decisions in times of crisis. Candor allows leaders to remain open to feedback and growth, ensuring that decisions are made in the organization's best interests. Lastly, accountability reinforces responsibility and commitment, encouraging a culture of reliability and excellence. Together, these core values empower leaders to navigate challenges with resilience and competence, inspiring those they lead to strive towards a shared vision and a sustainable future. As we continue to explore and define leadership in an ever-changing world, these timeless values will remain central to the pursuit of meaningful and impactful leadership.

PatrickJester.com

ABOUT THE AUTHOR

A U.S. Army veteran and former Blackhawk crew chief, Patrick is the driving force behind Blackthorn Consulting Group, Inc., delivering transformative solutions in quality management systems and training. As a Lead Assessor for ISO/IEC 17025 Calibration Laboratories, an ASQ Certified Quality Auditor, NCSLI Board Secretary, and Chair of ASQ's Measurement Quality Division, he helps companies achieve excellence.

With a Juris Doctor from Southern University Law Center, Patrick is an advocate for leadership and strategic growth. His career spans two decades in metrology, quality, and legal compliance, making him a sought-after speaker and mentor in the industry.

A lifelong learner and passionate leader, Patrick draws inspiration from John C. Maxwell and his Christian faith. He has been married to his wife Carol since 2004 and is a proud father of four.

ACKNOWLEDGEMENTS

This book represents a labor of love and passion, and I owe a debt of gratitude to many individuals who have supported me throughout this journey.

G.T. Michelli, Jr., you are my hero. From the outset of this project, your life's work served as an inspiration, and you continue to embody every core value I hold dear.

Shane Schexnayder, your unwavering support over the past few years has preserved my sanity. You were there with me when I first presented the initial material from this book, offering candid critiques that helped refine my work each time.

Heather A. Wade, Henry Zumbrun, and Dilip Shah, you have been with me on the Core Values of Leadership journey since the beginning. Your professional mentorship is invaluable, and I am honored to call each of you a friend.

Aysegul Konu, your candor and incredible support have been invaluable, and I am eternally grateful.

To the team that stood with me through thick and thin! John Harris, Ben "B.J." Bement, Bill Usher, and Adam Bell, you are my Prayer Warriors!

To my brother, Larry Jester, your encouragement and daily insights into leadership have been indispensable. You are a true American hero, operating behind the scenes with the selflessness of a dedicated Operations Officer.

To all the editors, pre-readers, publisher, marketing and everyone who helped me get the book completed.

I am deeply honored by each of you taking the time to offer your wisdom and insight during the writing of this.

REFERENCES

[1] https://languages.oup.com/google-dictionary-en/value (n.d.).

[2] https://languages.oup.com/google-dictionary-en/integrity (n.d.).

[3] Garner & Garner, Garner's Dictionary of Legal Usage 2011

[4] Army Field Manual FM 22-100: The U.S. Army Leadership Field Manual. (n.d.).

[5] FMFM 1-0 Marine Corps Manual. (n.d.).

[6] A Profession of Arms: Our Core Values – U.S. Air Force. (n.d.).

[7] The 21 Irrefutable Laws of Leadership: Follow Them and People Will Follow You. Thomas Nelson, 2007.

[8] Merriam-Webster. (n.d.). Accountability Definition & meaning. Merriam-Webster. https://www.merriam-webster.com/dictionary/accountability

[9] Drucker, P. F. (1974). Management - tasks, responsibilities, practices: (by) Peter F. Drucker. Harper and Row.

www.ingramcontent.com/pod-product-compliance
Lightning Source LLC
Chambersburg PA
CBHW060636210326
41520CB00010B/1629